World of Mammals

Foxes

by Adele Richardson

Consultant:
Marsha A. Sovada, Research Wildlife Biologist
Northern Prairie Wildlife Research Center
U.S. Geological Survey
Jamestown, North Dakota

Capstone press

Mankato, Minnesota

Bridgestone Books are published by Capstone Press,
151 Good Counsel Drive, P.O. Box 669, Mankato, Minnesota 56002.
www.capstonepress.com

Library of Congress Cataloging-in-Publication Data
Richardson, Adele, 1966–
    Foxes / by Adele Richardson.
    p. cm.—(Bridgestone books. World of mammals)
    Includes bibliographical references and index.
    ISBN-13: 978-0-7368-5416-0 (hardcover)
    ISBN-10: 07368-5416-9 (hardcover)
    1. Foxes—Juvenile literature. I. Title. II. Series: World of mammals.
QL737.C22R52 2006
599.775—dc22   2005018704

Summary: A brief introduction to foxes, discussing their characteristics, range, habitat, food, offspring, and
    dangers. Includes a range map, life cycle diagram, and amazing facts.

Editorial Credits
Katy Kudela, editor; Molly Nei, set designer; Kim Brown and Patrick D. Dentinger, book designers;
    Wanda Winch, photo researcher; Scott Thoms, photo editor; Tami Collins, life cycle illustrator;
    Nancy Steers, map illustrator

Photo Credits
Corbis/Kennan Ward, 18; Erwin and Peggy Bauer, 12; McDonald Wildlife Photography/Joe McDonald,
6; Nature Picture Library/Graham Hatherley, 10; Nature Picture Library/T. J. Rich, 16; SuperStock/Age
Fotostock, 1; Tom and Pat Leeson, cover, 4, 20

1 2 3 4 5 6 11 10 09 08 07 06

Table of Contents

Foxes

Foxes bark just like dogs. Despite their doglike features, most people wouldn't want a fox as a pet. Foxes are not tame like household dogs.

Foxes are members of the dog family. Wolves and coyotes are other wild animals in the dog family.

The dog family belongs to a large group of animals called **mammals**. Mammals have backbones and fur. As newborns, they drink their mother's milk.

◄ A red fox stops to catch a scent on the edge of a lake. Like dogs, foxes have a sharp sense of smell.

What Foxes Look Like

Some people think foxes look like small dogs. But the tails of foxes are bushier than those of most dogs.

Foxes have red, orange, gray, white, or tan fur. Their fur keeps them warm and helps them blend in with their surroundings.

Male and female foxes look alike. Male foxes, called dogs, grow up to 27 inches (69 centimeters) long. Female foxes are slightly smaller in size. They are called vixens.

◀ A fox's bushy tail is called a brush.

Fox Range Map

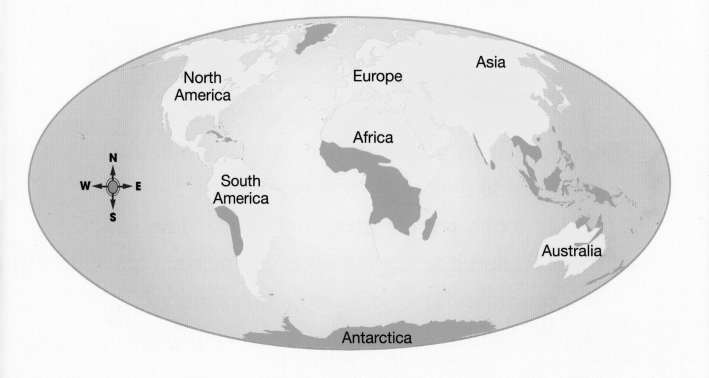

| | **Where Foxes Live** |

Foxes in the World

Foxes live all over the world. They make their homes on every continent except Antarctica. They live all the way from the northern tip of Greenland to the southern part of Australia.

In North America, there are six **species** of fox. These animals are the arctic fox, red fox, kit fox, swift fox, gray fox, and island fox. The red fox is the most common species in North America.

Fox Habitats

Foxes live in all kinds of habitats from hot, barren earth to cold, frozen plains. The fennec fox lives in sandy deserts. The arctic fox roams the icy tundra. Red foxes live in thick forests and in grassy meadows.

Fox families live and hunt in **territories**. They leave a scent on trees and bushes to mark their area. The scent lets other foxes know that a fox family already lives and hunts there.

◄ Fennec foxes make their homes in hot deserts.

What Foxes Eat

Foxes aren't fussy about what they eat. They eat insects, fruits, and seeds. They hunt mice, rabbits, and frogs. Foxes are called **omnivores** because they eat both plants and animals.

Foxes usually hunt alone and at night. They have good night vision and sharp hearing. A fox's **prey** is usually unaware that it is about to become a snack. A fox quietly sneaks up on its prey. Once the prey is close, the fox pounces.

◀ A gray fox nibbles on wild berries in a forest.

The Life Cycle of a Fox

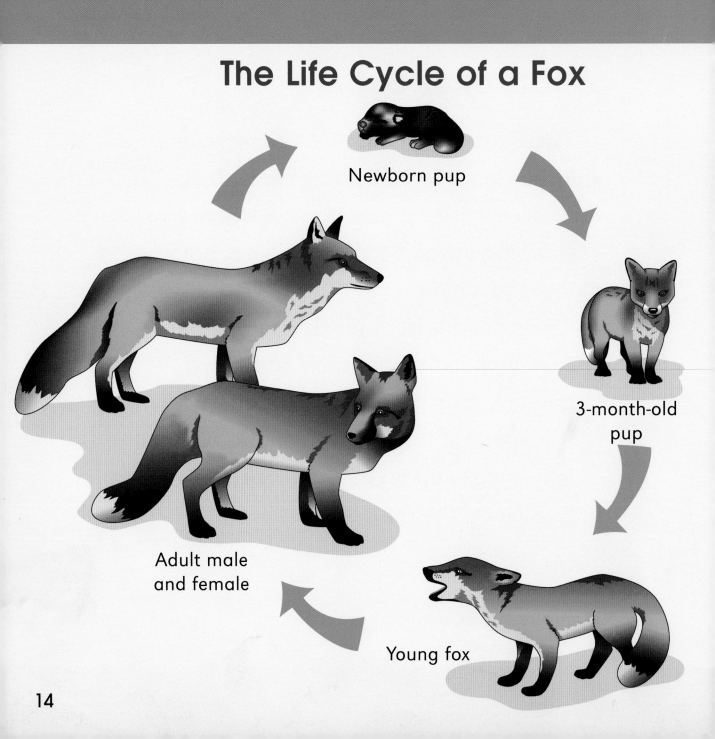

Newborn pup

3-month-old pup

Young fox

Adult male and female

Producing Young

Male and female foxes usually **mate** during the winter months. After mating, the pair searches for a **den**. In the spring, the mother fox gives birth to two to eight live young.

Newborn foxes are called pups, cubs, or kits. Pups stay close to their parents in the den. They drink their mother's milk until they are about 5 weeks old.

Growing Up

After the first month, pups begin to explore the world outside of their den. They learn to hunt. They practice hunting skills by pouncing on insects.

At first, fox parents bring their pups food. Pups begin to hunt for their own food when they are about 3 months old.

Most young foxes can take care of themselves when they are 6 months old. Then they leave the family's den and find their own territories.

◀ Fox mothers keep guard over their pups and den.

Dangers to Foxes

Adult foxes have few enemies. But coyotes, hawks, and other **predators** hunt pups. Fox parents fight off predators to keep their pups safe.

People are a danger to all foxes. Some hunters kill foxes for their soft fur. Other people build on land where foxes live. These building projects push foxes from their homes. Foxes stay safe by moving to new territories. But not many wilderness areas remain.

◄ Roads and highways often run through fox habitats.

Amazing Facts about Foxes

- Arctic foxes have brown or gray fur in the summer. In the winter, their fur turns white to blend in with the snow.
- Fennec foxes can hear large insects walk across the sand.
- Gray foxes are the only members of the dog family that can climb trees.
- Foxes save food for later. They drop extra food into small holes they dig in the ground. They go back later to eat the stored food.

◄ Arctic foxes make their homes on the icy tundra. They have thick fur to keep them warm in freezing wind and snow.

Glossary

den (DEN)—the place where a wild animal lives; a fox den can be a hollow log, cave, or hole in the ground.

mammal (MAM-uhl)—a warm-blooded animal that has a backbone; female mammals feed milk to their young.

mate (MAYT)—to join together to produce young

omnivore (OM-nuh-vor)—an animal that eats both plants and animals

predator (PRED-uh-tur)—an animal that hunts other animals for food

prey (PRAY)—an animal hunted by another animal for food

species (SPEE-sheez)—a group of animals or plants that share common characteristics

territory (TER-uh-tor-ee)—an area of land that an animal claims as its own to live and hunt in

Read More

Levine, Michelle. *Red Foxes.* Pull Ahead Books. Minneapolis: Lerner, 2004.

Swanson, Diane. *Foxes.* Welcome to the World of Animals. Milwaukee: Gareth Stevens, 2003.

Internet Sites

FactHound offers a safe, fun way to find Internet sites related to this book. All of the sites on FactHound have been researched by our staff.

Here's how:
1. Visit *www.facthound.com*
2. Type in this special code **0736854169** for age-appropriate sites. Or enter a search word related to this book for a more general search.
3. Click on the **Fetch It** button.

FactHound will fetch the best sites for you!

Index